LAUNCH YOUR PROFESSIONAL SPEAKING CAREER

A Kingdom Speaker's Handbook To Increase Your Impact, Income and Influence

CRYSTAL S. DAYE

Award Winning Author

LAUNCH YOUR PROFESSIONAL SPEAKING CAREER. Copyright © 2025. Crystal Daye. All Rights Reserved.

Printed in the United States of America.

No portion of this book may be reproduced, stored in a retrieval system, or transmitted in any form or by any means, except for brief quotations in printed reviews, without the prior written permission of DayeLight Publishers.

DAYELight
PUBLISHERS

ISBN: 978-1-966723-39-4 (paperback)

Table of
CONTENTS

Introduction 1
A Special Gift For You 3
Dear Kingdom Speaker 4

Part 1: The Calling 7

Chapter 1: ANSWER THE CALL TO SPEAK 8
What To Do If You Feel Called To Speak 8
What Makes You A Kingdom Speaker? 9
Should A Christian Seek A Platform? 10
Why Authors Should Speak 10
Why Should Speakers Become Authors? 11
A Note from The Author 12

Chapter 2: PUBLIC SPEAKING VS PROFESSIONAL SPEAKING ... 15
Who Is a Public Speaker? 15
Who Is a Professional Speaker? 15
The Mindset Shift From Public to Professional 16
The Practical Differences: What Separates The Two 17
8 Powerful Affirmations For Kingdom Speakers 18

Chapter 3: SPEAKING MINISTRY VS SPEAKING BUSINESS 22
Am I Called Primarily to Ministry Settings or Marketplace Settings? .. 22
What Is a Speaking Ministry? 22
What Is a Speaking Business? 23
Can You Do Both? 24
Both Callings Are Kingdom Work 24
Types Of Speakers 28
Speaker Type Mini Quiz 29

Part 2: The Clarity 32

Chapter 4: CLARIFY YOUR PURPOSE & POSITIONING 33
- Identify Your Why 33
- Define Your Mission 33
- Mission Statement Template: 34
- Define Your Vision 34
- Goal-Setting for Professional Speakers 34

Chapter 5: BUILDING YOUR SPEAKER BRAND 39
- What Is a Speaker Brand? 39
- The Pillars of a Speaker Brand 39
- Clarify Your Ideal Audience 40
- Develop Your Speaking Platform 40
- Essential Tools for Speakers 41

Part 3: The Craft 44

Chapter 6: DEVELOP YOUR SIGNATURE SPEECH 45
- What Is a Signature Speech 45
- Choosing Your Speaking Topics 45
- Ways to Use Your Signature Talk 46
- The Foundation of Every Great Speech 46
- Writing & Refining Your Speech 47
- Deliver with Confidence 47
- Naming & Packaging Your Signature Talk 47
- Types of Speaking Platforms 47

Chapter 7: THE ART OF STORYTELLING 51
- Why Storytelling Matters 51
- How to Overcome the Insecurities to Speak Boldly 51
- How to Use Storytelling as a Speaker 52
- The 3V Storytelling Framework 52
- The Four Core Phases of the 3V Story: 52
- How to Use the 3V Story in Your Talks 55
- Build Your Story Bank 55

Categories to Include in Your Story Bank: 55
Tips for Impactful Storytelling 55
Practice, Polish and Protect Your Story 56

Part 4: The Cashflow 59

Chapter 8: VISIBILITY AS A PROFESSIONAL SPEAKER 60

Why Visibility Matters 60
How to Position Yourself for Visibility 60
The 5 Pillars of Visibility for Kingdom Speakers 61
How to Find Speaking Engagements (Get Your First Speaking Gig) 62
How to Partner with Event Planners 63
How to Track & Steward Opportunities 63

Chapter 9: MONETIZATION AS A PROFESSIONAL SPEAKER 67

The Speaker Business Flow 67
How to Set Fees and Increase Your Earnings as a Speaker 68
Using Speaking to Build Your Business 68
Creating Multiple Streams of Income as a Speaker 69
Speaking for Free vs Speaking for a Fee 69
When to Speak for Free (Strategically) 69
How to Transition from Free to Fee 70
How to Sell From the Stage Authentically 70
How to Steward Your Finances as a Speaker 70

Chapter 10: HOW TO SELL YOUR BOOKS AS A SPEAKER 73

The Connection Between Speaking and Selling 73
Positioning Your Book in Your Talk 73
How to Sell Books Before, During, and After You Speak 74
Packaging Your Book With Your Speaking Offers 74
How to Use Your Book to Book More Speaking Gigs 75
Practical Tips for On-the-Spot Sales 75
What To Do If You Don't Have a Book Yet 75

Resources 80

Event Preparation Checklist 81
  Spiritual Preparation 81
  Message Preparation 81
  Brand & Materials 81
  Logistics & Personal Prep 81
  Engagement & Follow-Up 82
SWOT Analysis For Speakers 84
  Why Every Speaker Should Do a SWOT Analysis 84
90-Day Goal Planner For Speakers 86
  Books by Crystal Daye 93

Introduction

You've felt it—that gentle whisper, that sacred stirring deep in your spirit that says, *"You have something to say"*

Maybe it came while you were journaling, in worship, or through a friend who said, "Your story could really help someone." That's not coincidence—that's the holy nudge. And the fact that you're reading these words means you can't ignore it anymore.

Still, I know what's going through your mind:

Where do I start? What would I even say? Who would listen? Am I really qualified? And is it wrong to want to be paid for something that feels like ministry?

You're not alone. Every impact-driven communicator wrestles with these same questions. I certainly did. For years, I felt torn between serving God and sustaining myself. Between ministry and money. But here's what I discovered—you don't have to choose.

You can honor God and build a business that funds your vision. You can speak from the heart and earn income that supports your mission. You can inspire souls and create systems that make your message sustainable.

We are living in a time when people are searching for hope, direction and authenticity. The world doesn't need more noise—it needs more Kingdom voices. This is not the season to shrink back or disqualify yourself. The world needs your message.

I wasn't always confident or clear. My first speaking invitation came unexpectedly, and I was terrified. I had no speaker sheet, no signature talk, and no idea what to charge—so I didn't. I just showed up, spoke from the heart, and trusted God with the rest. That one act of obedience changed everything.

Doors began to open. Audiences grew. Opportunities increased. But more importantly, I learned how to steward my calling with both faith and strategy.

That's what this handbook is designed to help you do—turn your God-given message into movement and your calling into a confident speaking career that creates real impact.

So take a deep breath. The stage is waiting. The world is ready. And now—it's your time to rise.

Welcome to your Kingdom Speaking journey.

Let's launch your professional speaking career—together.

A Special Gift For You

As a thank you for purchasing this book, I've created a bonus resource area to help you on your speaking journey.

I know the process can sometimes feel overwhelming — trying to get booked, become more confident on stage, and grow your platform while staying true to your Kingdom purpose.

That's why I put together these exclusive bonuses to help you:

- Build your boldness and strengthen your faith as you answer the call to speak
- Gain clarity and structure so you can start showing up with confidence and consistency

Your bonuses include:

1. Empowered to Speak: A 5-Day Devotional for Women Called to Impact
2. 30-Day Launch Checklist for New & Emerging Speakers

Download your resources at bit.ly/empoweredtospeakresource

"Remember, you don't need to have it all figured out — you just need faith to start."

— Crystal Daye

Dear Kingdom Speaker

In writing this book, I felt the same mix of excitement and conviction I know many of you feel. Whether you are speaking in churches, conferences, schools, corporate offices or on social media, I truly believe the strategies in this handbook will help you grow your impact, influence and income.

But before we dive into the strategies and systems, I wanted to pause and speak to your spirit first.

As a Kingdom Speaker—someone who carries the message of Christ through your voice, your story, and your platform—your assignment is not just motivational; it's missional. You are not just called to speak; you are chosen to shift atmospheres and release hope through your words.

And that's why the journey won't always be easy. You will face resistance, doubt, and fear. Not just because you're a speaker, but because you're a Kingdom speaker.

Ephesians 6:12 reminds us that "we wrestle not against flesh and blood."

The moment you decide to use your voice to glorify God and transform lives, you declare war on darkness—and the enemy doesn't like that. But here's the truth: You've already won.

You have the full armor of God and the anointing of the Holy Spirit backing you. So while the process may stretch you, you are fully equipped for it.

Also, remember Matthew 6:33 reminds us to "seek first the Kingdom of God and His righteousness," and everything else—including your visibility, bookings, money, platform and resources—will follow.

So don't shrink back.

Don't compare yourself to the world's standards or chase platforms that compromise your values. Instead, show up with excellence, steward your gift well, and trust that the same God who called you will open the doors meant for you.

You may or may not become a viral speaker or stand on the world's biggest stages—but your obedience will change lives.

Dream big, prepare well and trust God with the outcome. Your voice is not just a sound, it's a solution.

With Faith,
Crystal Daye

Part 1

The Calling

Chapter 1
ANSWER THE CALL TO SPEAK

"You're not just called to speak — you're called to steward your story and serve through your voice." – C. Daye

There's a moment that comes to every messenger—an intersection where divine assignment meets human willingness. It's the moment when you realize that the story you've been carrying, the lessons you've learned through your trials, and the wisdom God has deposited in you are not just for your own benefit. They're meant to be shared.

That moment is your call to speaking.

But recognizing the call is only the beginning. The real question is: What will you do with it?

What To Do If You Feel Called To Speak

The call to speak rarely comes with clear instructions. It often starts as a whisper, a stirring, a quiet knowing that you have something important to say. You might be in a conversation when you think, "More people need to hear this." Or while journaling, God drops a message in your heart that feels too powerful to keep to yourself.

If you feel that call, here's what to do:

1. Acknowledge it: When God gives you a message, it's not pride—it's purpose. If you're questioning your worthiness, that's usually proof the calling is real.

2. Test it in community: Share your message at church, at a local event, or with friends. Notice the fruit. Are people moved? Are lives changing? The call is confirmed by transformation.

3. Invest in your gift: A calling is not an excuse to procrastinate or be lazy. Study, practice, learn from mentors. Your anointing opens doors, but your skill keeps you in the room.

4. Start where you are: You don't need a big platform. Speak wherever God opens the door—big or small.

5. Pray for direction: Ask God to guide your words, open the right doors, and close the wrong ones.

The call to speak is an invitation to partner with God—He provides the message, you provide the voice.

Don't overthink it. Don't delay it. Just answer the call.

What Makes You A Kingdom Speaker?

Not every speaker is a Kingdom speaker—and that's not judgment, it's distinction.

Speaking isn't just a career choice—it's a divine assignment. You carry a message from God that's meant to impact lives.

But being a Kingdom speaker doesn't mean quoting scriptures on every stage. Kingdom is about representing Heaven's values—excellence, integrity, and influence—wherever you speak.

A Kingdom speaker speaks for transformation, not just information. You don't aim to impress—you speak to heal and inspire lasting change.

You walk in integrity, honor your word, prepare well, and treat every platform—big or small—with excellence.

You practice stewardship, knowing your platform, opportunities, and income are gifts from God to be managed wisely.

And you blend purpose and profit, understanding that ministry and money are not enemies.

You're not called to stay within the church walls but to influence culture with truth and grace.

When you know what it means to be a Kingdom speaker, you don't just share words—you carry a message with eternal weight.

Should A Christian Seek A Platform?

It's not about seeking—it's about stewardship.

Many Christians wrestle with this question: If God wants to elevate me, won't He do it Himself? Yes—but elevation often meets preparation. God gives you the message, but He also expects you to steward it.

Seeking a platform is not the same as seeking fame. Fame is about ego—wanting to be seen and celebrated. Platform is about obedience—positioning your message where it can reach the people God called you to serve.

Hiding your gift out of fear or false humility doesn't glorify God. Jesus said, "Let your light shine before others." (Matthew 5:16)

Your platform is not about you being seen—it's about making sure the message God placed in you is seen.

So ask yourself: Am I seeking attention, or am I stewarding my assignment?

That answer will reveal whether your pursuit is pride or purpose.

Why Authors Should Speak

Your book needs your voice. Writing reaches minds but speaking reaches hearts. Readers connect more deeply when they can hear your passion and see your conviction.

Speaking brings your message to life—it helps audiences feel your story, not just read it. And when people connect with you, they naturally want to buy your book, share it, and follow your work.

Here's why every author should be speaking:

- ✓ Visibility: Every stage puts you in front of new audiences who may have never heard of you or your book;
- ✓ Credibility: Speaking positions you as an authority—people trust and remember experts they've seen and heard;
- ✓ Connection: Your energy and authenticity can't always be captured on a page, but they shine from the stage;
- ✓ Sales: Speakers sell more books because audiences want to go deeper with the message that moved them;

- ✓ Opportunities: Speaking leads to media features, podcast invites, and collaborations that grow your reach;
- ✓ Impact: God didn't just call you to w;rite—He called you to proclaim. Speaking ensures your message multiplies
- ✓ Income: Beyond book sales, speaking creates new income streams—keynotes, workshops, coaching, and more.

If you've written a book but aren't speaking yet, you're leaving opportunity and impact on the table. Your book is your business card, and your voice is your amplifier. Together, they expand your influence far beyond what words on a page can do.

Why Should Speakers Become Authors?

Now let's flip the question. If you're a speaker who hasn't yet written a book, you need to understand this: Your voice needs a written form.

Speaking is powerful—but temporary. Your words fade once the event ends. A book gives your message permanence. It allows your story, wisdom, and lessons to keep speaking long after you've left the stage.

Here's why every speaker should write a book:

- ✓ Clarity: Writing refines your message. It forces you to organize your thoughts and communicate with precision;
- ✓ Reach: You can only be in one room at a time—but your book can reach thousands around the world;
- ✓ Income: Book sales create passive income that complements your speaking fees;
- ✓ Legacy: Events end, but books endure. They keep impacting lives for generations;
- ✓ Credibility: "Author" instantly elevates your authority—planners, media, and clients take you more seriously;
- ✓ Depth: Writing helps you understand your message more deeply, making you a stronger, more effective communicator.

The most successful speakers are also authors because they understand the synergy—books sell talks, and talks sell books.

If you're serious about building long-term influence, writing a book isn't optional—it's essential.

A Note from The Author

As you read this, maybe you already sense that it's time to turn your message into a book. That's exactly why DayeLight Publishers exists—to help Kingdom authors, speakers, and coaches bring their stories to life and build impact-driven brands that shine.

Since 2017, the DayeLight team, led by CEO Crystal Daye has helped hundreds of faith-based authors write, publish, promote and monetize books that change lives and reach nations.

If you're a speaker ready to write your first (or next) book, DayeLight Publishers would be honored to guide you through the process from idea to impact.

Learn more at www.dayelightpublishers.com

 **Reflection Questions**

Take a few quiet moments to think and write your answers.

1. When did you first feel called to speak?

2. What fears or doubts are holding you back?

3. What makes you a Kingdom speaker?

4. How can speaking or writing expand your impact?

5. How do you define your success?

Chapter 2
PUBLIC SPEAKING VS PROFESSIONAL SPEAKING

"The difference between a public speaker and a professional speaker is not talent—it's intentionality, systems and the courage to value your gift" – C. Daye

One of the biggest misconceptions in the speaking world is that all speakers are the same. People often use "public speaker" and "professional speaker" interchangeably — but they are not the same. Understanding the difference will shape your positioning, pricing, brand, and long-term success.

Who Is a Public Speaker?

A public speaker is anyone who speaks in public — at church, work, PTA meetings, networking events, or community programs.

Public speaking is usually:

- Unpaid or low-paid
- Informal and lightly prepared
- Occasional or spontaneous
- Focused on sharing, not selling
- Limited to familiar audiences

There is nothing wrong with public speaking; many Kingdom speakers start here. But it is not designed to sustain a speaking career.

Who Is a Professional Speaker?

A professional speaker treats speaking as a business and a calling.

This means that they:

- Charge for their expertise

- Prepare and rehearse with excellence
- Speak regularly and intentionally
- Have business systems (website, speaker sheet, contracts, media kit)
- Market themselves strategically
- Leverage multiple income streams (books, coaching, workshops, etc.)
- Reach audiences beyond their immediate community

If your goal is to build a sustainable speaking career—one that creates lasting impact and consistent income—you must move from public speaking to professional speaking.

The Mindset Shift From Public to Professional

Moving from public speaker to professional speaker starts with a mindset shift. It's not just what you do—it's how you think.

1. From Volunteer → Business Owner

You stop treating speaking like a hobby and begin valuing your time, expertise, and preparation. Charging doesn't make you less spiritual—it makes you sustainable.

2. From Casual → Excellent

No more "winging it." Professional speakers prepare, rehearse, and show up with excellence every time.

3. From Passive → Proactive

Public speakers wait for invitations. Professionals create opportunities—pitching, networking, and building relationships.

4. From "What I Want to Say" → "What They Need to Hear"

You tailor your message to serve the audience, not yourself.

5. From One-Time Moments → Long-Term Relationships

Every stage becomes a doorway to deeper connection, clients, and ongoing opportunities.

6. From Hidden → Visible

Visibility isn't vanity—it's stewardship. If people don't know you exist, they can't book you.

Can You Be Both? - Yes. You can still serve for free when it's strategic or meaningful—but you no longer allow people to exploit your gift. You choose intentionally when to sow and when to charge.

The Practical Differences: What Separates The Two

Let's get practical. Here's a side-by-side comparison of public speakers versus professional speakers:

Branding

- Public Speaker: No formal brand. May not even have a website or professional presence online.
- Professional Speaker: Clear, consistent brand identity. Professional website, social media presence, and marketing materials that position them as an expert.

Speaking Fee

- Public Speaker: Free or low honorarium
- Professional Speaker: Strategic fee structure and scaling based on audience size, event type, and value delivered.

Booking Process

- Public Speaker: Informal. "Just let me know the date and I'll be there."
- Professional Speaker: Formal. Contract, deposit, clear expectations, technical rider, travel arrangements handled professionally.

Content Development

- Public Speaker: Creates new content for each event. No signature speech.
- Professional Speaker: Has a signature speech or suite of core messages that have been tested, refined, and proven to produce results.

Marketing Materials

- Public Speaker: Maybe a basic bio. No speaker sheet or demo video.
- Professional Speaker: Complete media kit including speaker sheet, professional photos, demo video, testimonials, and topic descriptions.

Preparation
- Public Speaker: Shows up and speaks from the heart. Minimal preparation.
- Professional Speaker: Rehearses, customizes content for the audience, arrives early to check equipment, and delivers with polish and precision.

Follow-Up
- Public Speaker: Thanks the host and moves on.
- Professional Speaker: Collects testimonials, takes professional photos/video, requests referrals, adds attendees to email list, and leverages the event for future opportunities.

Business Operations
- Public Speaker: No formal business structure. No tracking of expenses, income, or speaking metrics.
- Professional Speaker: Registered business, tracks all financials, files taxes appropriately, and manages their speaking career as a legitimate enterprise.

Long-Term Strategy
- Public Speaker: Reacts to opportunities as they come.
- Professional Speaker: Proactively builds a speaking calendar 6-12 months in advance, pursues strategic partnerships, and creates multiple income streams.

8 Powerful Affirmations For Kingdom Speakers

Words have power. These affirmations are rooted in Scripture and designed to renew your mind as you step into your role as a Kingdom speaker.

1. "I am called and equipped to speak life into others."

"Before I formed you in the womb I knew you, before you were born I set you apart; I appointed you as a prophet to the nations." – Jeremiah 1:5

2. "My words carry the power to transform lives."

"Death and life are in the power of the tongue, and those who love it will eat its fruit." – Proverbs 18:21

3. "I am worthy of compensation for the value I bring."

"The worker deserves his wages." – 1 Timothy 5:18

4. "I steward my gift with excellence and integrity."

"Whatever you do, work at it with all your heart, as working for the Lord, not for human masters." – Colossians 3:23

5. "God opens doors for me that no one can shut."

"What he opens no one can shut, and what he shuts no one can open." – Revelation 3:7

6. "I am not in competition with anyone; I have a unique message."

"For we are God's handiwork, created in Christ Jesus to do good works, which God prepared in advance for us to do." – Ephesians 2:10

7. "I build a sustainable business that honors God and serves people."

"Plans fail for lack of counsel, but with many advisers they succeed." – Proverbs 15:22

8. "I boldly share my message without fear or apology."

"For God has not given us a spirit of fear, but of power and of love and of a sound mind." – 2 Timothy 1:7

Reflection Questions

1. How have I been viewing myself—as a public speaker or a professional speaker—and how is that affecting the way I show up?'

2. What mindset shift do I need to make (value, excellence, visibility, fully into professionalism?

3. What fears or beliefs have been keeping me hidden instead of visible, and how can I replace them with truth?

Chapter 3
SPEAKING MINISTRY VS SPEAKING BUSINESS

"Your calling determines your primary platform, but your message can travel anywhere." – C. Daye

Am I Called Primarily to Ministry Settings or Marketplace Settings?

One of the most important questions you'll answer as a Kingdom speaker is this: ***Am I called primarily to ministry settings or marketplace settings?***

Notice, this isn't about being more spiritual or more business-minded. It's not about whether you love God more or money more. Those are false dichotomies that keep Kingdom speakers confused and stuck.

The real question is about **assignment**—where is God calling you to predominantly operate?

Understanding the difference between a **speaking ministry** and a **speaking business** will bring:

- **Clarity** to your strategy
- **Focus** to your marketing
- **Confidence** to your calling

What Is a Speaking Ministry?

A **speaking ministry** is built around serving primarily in **church and religious contexts.** Your audience is the Body of Christ—churches, women's and men's ministries, Christian conferences, denominational gatherings, ministry leadership events, and faith-based retreats.

If you're called to a speaking ministry, your calendar might include:

- Sunday morning services
- Women's conferences at local churches

- Youth group events
- Ministry leader trainings
- Christian retreat centers
- Denominational conventions
- Faith-based nonprofit gatherings

Your content is **mostly biblical.** You preach, teach Scripture, lead Bible studies, and offer spiritual direction. Your ultimate goal is to **edify believers, equip the saints, and strengthen the Church.**

If you feel God has called you to this lane, you're in good company. The Church desperately needs anointed communicators who can rightly divide the Word of truth and shepherd God's people with wisdom and compassion.

What Is a Speaking Business?

A **speaking business** is built around serving primarily in the **marketplace and general audience contexts.** Your audience extends beyond the church walls — corporations, conferences, schools, nonprofits, community organizations, and what some might call "secular" settings.

If you're called to a speaking business, your calendar might include:

- Corporate leadership conferences
- Professional development workshops
- Industry conventions
- University and college events
- TEDx or local community talks
- Civic forums and networking events
- Nonprofit fundraisers or galas
- General conferences on topics like wellness, entrepreneurship, or personal growth

Your content is **Kingdom-minded but not overtly religious**. You teach on leadership, mindset, purpose, relationships, business strategy, or resilience from a **biblical worldview**, yet your message is packaged for diverse audiences.

You are, in essence, **a missionary in the marketplace**—bringing Kingdom principles to spaces where traditional ministry language may not always fit. This doesn't mean you hide your faith; it means you're strategic about how and when you share it.

Building a speaking business requires **entrepreneurial skills**—marketing, branding, networking, and positioning your message so it resonates with event planners, decision-makers, and general audiences while maintaining your Kingdom foundation.

Can You Do Both?

Absolutely! Many Kingdom speakers operate in both ministry and marketplace spaces. But here's the key — you must know which one is your **primary focus**.

Trying to build equal momentum in both simultaneously often leads to confusion, diluted branding, and missed opportunities. Each arena values different things.

- Churches look for **Bible teachers**
- Corporations look for **thought leaders**
- Conferences look for **experts**

If you try to be everything to everyone, you'll end up resonating with no one.

Instead, **identify your primary calling** and build from there.

For example:

— A ministry speaker may focus on church and faith-based audiences but occasionally accept opportunities to speak at Christian schools or nonprofit fundraisers.
— A marketplace speaker may build their brand in corporate or entrepreneurial spaces, yet occasionally speak at church leadership or Christian business events.

Both Callings Are Kingdom Work

Let this be clear: **Ministry speakers are not more spiritual than marketplace speakers.**

If God has called you to preach in pulpits, that's holy work. If God has called you to speak in boardrooms, that's equally holy work.

The Kingdom needs both. We need anointed Bible teachers who strengthen the saints. We also need Kingdom ambassadors who carry God's wisdom into the culture, showing that biblical principles work everywhere.

Don't let anyone make you feel guilty or inferior for the space God assigned you to. Whether you're teaching at a women's retreat or keynoting a business summit, you are on divine assignment.

The question isn't which calling is better—the question is which calling is yours?

"Ministry or marketplace, pulpit or podium—wherever God sends you is sacred ground. Walk confidently in your assignment."

 **Reflection Questions**

1. Where do I feel most alive when speaking?

2. What audience keeps showing up in my vision?

3. What type of content excites me most?

4. What opportunities keep opening for me?

5. Where can I create the most Kingdom impact?

Types Of Speakers

Inspirational Speaker

Shares personal stories of overcoming challenges to uplift and encourage others. Example: A survivor who shares how they turned pain into purpose to inspire others to keep going.

Ideal For: Faith-based events, empowerment conferences, women's retreats. Like: Crystal Daye, Lisa Nichols and Nick Vujicic

Informational Speaker

Teaches, trains, or educates audiences on a specific topic or skill, offering clear frameworks and actionable strategies. Example: A business coach teaching "How to Build Your Author Brand Online."

Ideal For: Corporate workshops, webinars, and professional training sessions. Like: John Maxwell, Amy Porterfield and Myron Golden

Entertaining Speaker

Blends humor, storytelling, or performance to connect and engage. Example: A storyteller who uses comedy and real-life lessons to inspire resilience.

Ideal For: Conferences, youth events, galas, being a Master of Ceremonies (MC)/host and retreats Like: Steve Harvey, Tishauna Mullings and Michael Jr.

Motivational Speaker

Moves audiences to action. They don't just inspire—they ignite the space and the heart of their audience. Example: A speaker challenging entrepreneurs to overcome fear and take bold steps toward purpose.

Ideal for: Corporate events, leadership conferences, personal development summits and schools.

Like: Deshauna Barber, Eric Thomas and Les Brown

Preacher Speaker

Combines biblical truth with motivational storytelling. They inspire spiritual growth & faith. Example: A minister teaching "Faith Over Fear" using biblical stories and real-life application.

Ideal For: Church conferences, youth crusades, and Christian women's events Like: Carla Dunar, Priscilla Shirer and Sarah Jakes-Roberts

Activist Speaker

These speakers use their platform to raise awareness, challenge systems, or empower change in social or cultural issues. Example: A speaker addressing gender equality, education reform, or youth empowerment.

Ideal For: Nonprofit events, youth conferences, social campaigns.

Like: Malala Yousafzai and Mutabaruka

Celebrity Speaker

Uses their public influence or success story to inspire and inform others. Their credibility comes from personal achievements. Example: A known author, athlete, or media personality sharing leadership or success lessons.

Ideal For: Large conferences, brand events, or fundraising galas.

Like: Terri Karelle, Lisa Hanna, and Viola Davis

No matter your speaking style, remember every type of speaker has a unique audience, and every message has an appointed reach. Your responsibility is to discern your lane, refine your delivery, and serve faithfully where God has called you.

"Your voice doesn't have to sound like anyone else's — it just has to be obedient."

Speaker Type Mini Quiz

Take a moment to reflect and circle the statements that sound most like you:

1. When I speak, my biggest desire is to...

    A. Encourage and uplift people through my personal story.

B. Teach practical strategies that help people grow.
   C. Make people laugh, smile, and feel connected.
   D. Push past fear and go after their dreams.
   E. Help people grow spiritually and deepen their faith.
   F. Raise awareness and spark change around important issues.
   G. Share insights from my success or platform to inspire others.

2. My audience usually says I help them…

   A. Feel hope again.
   B. Learn something new and useful.
   C. See life from a lighter, joyful perspective.
   D. Challenge people to take bold action.
   E. Strengthen their relationship with God.
   F. Think critically and stand for justice.
   G. Believe they can achieve greatness too.

3. The setting I'm most comfortable in is…

   A. Women's retreats or empowerment events.
   B. Workshops, webinars, or training sessions.
   C. Youth events, open mics, or social gatherings.
   D. Leadership conferences or school assemblies.
   E. Church services, ministry events, or crusades.
   F. Social campaigns or nonprofit events.
   G. Media panels, red carpets, or brand events.

4. If I could summarize my message in one phrase, it would be…

   A. "Your pain has purpose."
   B. "Knowledge is power."
   C. "Laughter heals."
   D. "You have what it takes."
   E. "Faith conquers fear."
   F. "Change starts with courage."
   G. "Your influence is your impact."

Your Results:

Mostly A's: Inspirational Speaker
Mostly B's: Informational Speaker

Mostly C's: Entertaining Speaker
Mostly D's: Motivational Speaker
Mostly E's: Preacher Speaker
Mostly F's: Activist Speaker
Mostly G's: Celebrity Speaker

Part 2

The Clarity

Chapter 4
CLARIFY YOUR PURPOSE & POSITIONING

"This isn't just about getting booked– it's about walking boldly in your assignment to reach millions and represent the kingdom with excellence ."- C.Daye

Identify Your Why

You can't reach millions if you haven't first reached clarity about why you're called to speak. Every great message begins with a meaningful motivation. If you don't know why you do what you do, you'll get distracted by every opportunity that shows up.

Your "why" is the fire that fuels your focus. It keeps you grounded when doors don't open as fast as you hoped and reminds you that this isn't about fame — it's about faithfulness.

"When your 'why' is anchored in impact, your words will always find the right audience."

Ask yourself:

- Why has God called me to speak?
- What do I want people to think, feel, or do after hearing me? What transformation do I hope my story brings?

When your **why** is clear, your message becomes powerful.

Define Your Mission

Your **mission** defines what you do, who you serve, and how you serve them—right now. It's the practical expression of your purpose in this season. Your mission brings focus to your daily actions. It guides what you say yes to and gives direction to your speaking goals.

Mission Statement Template:

"I help _____ to _____ so they can __."

Examples:

"I help women of faith overcome self-doubt so they can confidently walk in their God-given purpose."

"I help young professionals discover their unique gifts so they can lead and live with impact."

Define Your Vision

Your vision paints the bigger picture, where you're going and the legacy you're building through your message. It's the long-term impact you want your voice to have in the world.

Vision Statement Template:

"My vision is to see a world where _____ through __."

Examples:

"My vision is to see a world where women walk boldly in their purpose through faith and mentorship."

"My vision is to see families restored and healed through Christ-centered communication."

Your vision is the **destination**; Your mission is the **roadmap**.

Goal-Setting for Professional Speakers

Once you've defined your purpose, mission, and vision, it's time to set intentional goals that help you grow as a speaker.

There are four types of goals every speaker should set:

❖ **Purpose Goals** – Your Why: The reason behind your message.

- ❖ Example: *"To speak in spaces where faith and purpose intersect."*

- ❖ **Performance Goals** – *Your Skill & Delivery: Becoming a more confident and effective communicator.*
- ❖ Example: *"Eliminate filler words ('um,' 'you know') by practicing weekly."*

- ❖ **Profit Goals** – *Your Income & Opportunities: Expanding your reach and earning potential.*
- ❖ Example: *"Book 5 paid speaking engagements this year."*

- ❖ **Platform Goals** – *Your Impact & Influence: Increasing your visibility and consistency as a speaker.*
- ❖ Example: *"Speak at three new organizations or conferences this quarter."*

VISION BOARD

 **Reflection Questions**

1. Why do I feel called to speak?

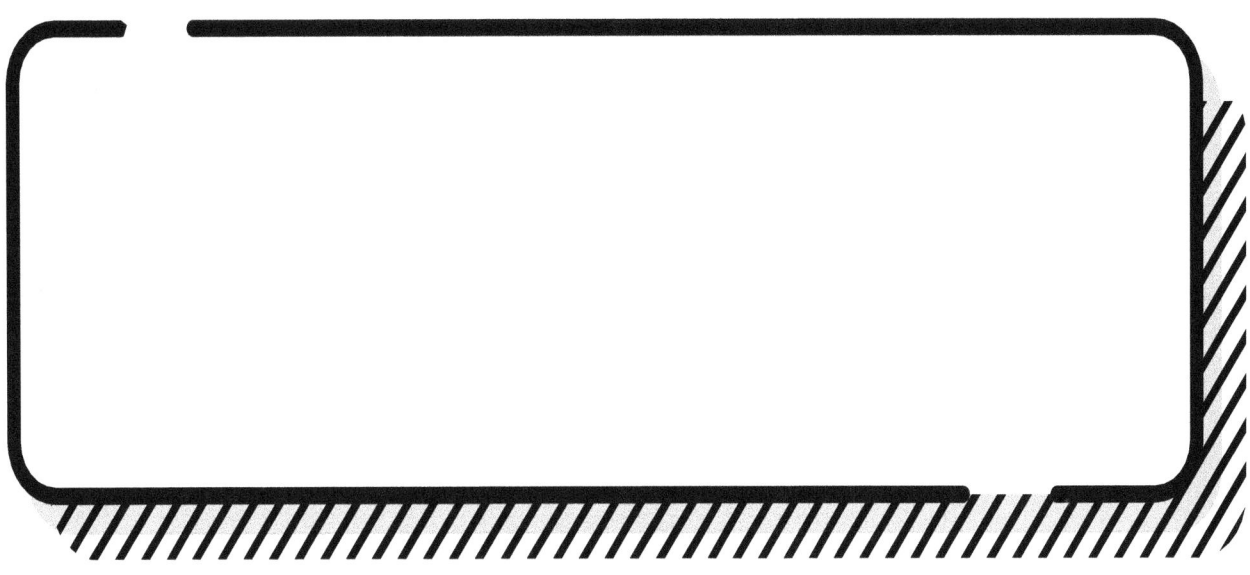

2. What problem does my message help people solve?

3. What 3 speaking goals will I focus on this year?

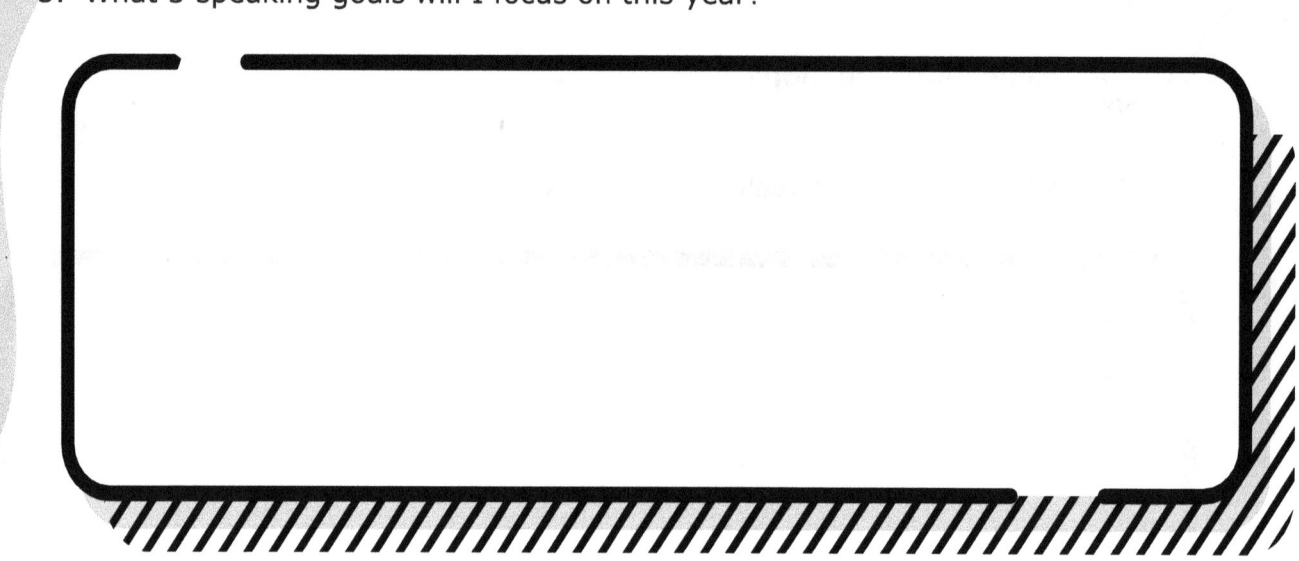

"When you are clear about your why, confident in your mission, and consistent in your message — doors don't just open, they align."
— *Crystal Daye*

Chapter 5
BUILDING YOUR SPEAKER BRAND

"Your brand isn't your logo—it's your voice, values and vibe. It's how people experience your message before you ever walk on stage" – C. Daye

What Is a Speaker Brand?

This is the consistent perception people have of who you are, what you stand for, and the transformation you create through your message.

It includes:

- Identity: your authentic story, personality, and voice
- Impact: the transformation your message brings
- Image: how you visually and verbally present that message to the world

"A strong brand makes you recognizable. A purpose-driven brand makes you unforgettable."

The Pillars of a Speaker Brand

These are the building blocks your readers can apply:

1. Message – Your signature story and key themes. Example: Faith & Purpose, Mindset & Confidence, Storytelling & Healing.
    a) What are 2-3 core topics you want to be known for?

2. Voice – Your tone, energy, and communication style.
    b) Are you bold and fiery? Soft and soulful? Practical and teaching-oriented?

3. Values – The principles that guide your brand. It helps your audience trust you.
    c) Integrity, faith, transformation, service, or empowerment.

4. Visuals – The look that supports your message. Emphasize consistency across all materials (slides, flyers, social media).
    d) Professional photos, color palette, and typography that feel aligned with your voice

(faith-based, bold, or serene).

5. Vibe – The emotional connection people feel.
    e) Ask: What do I want people to experience when they encounter me — peace, motivation, hope, or empowerment?

Clarify Your Ideal Audience

One of the biggest mistakes new speakers make is trying to speak to everyone. When your message is for everyone, it connects with no one.

The more specific you are about who you serve, the more powerful your message becomes. God has assigned you to a particular group of people—those who will hear your voice and experience transformation because of it.

Questions to Ask Yourself:

- What is the main topic you will speak on?
- Who do you feel called to speak to?
- What problem are you solving for your audience?
- Who can relate to your story?
- What is the major outcome you want them to experience after hearing you?
- What do you want to be known for?

"Your audience is your assignment. When you know who you're called to, you'll know how to show up."

Develop Your Speaking Platform

Your speaking platform is the foundation that supports your message, credibility, and visibility. It's how people find you, connect with you, and invite you to share your story.

Think of it as the place where your message meets your audience. It can include live events, social media, podcasts, guest appearances, or digital resources that help you share your message consistently.

Practical Ways to Build Your Platform:

- Host live or virtual workshops on your core topics.
- Be a guest on podcasts or online summits.
- Create free resources that reflect your message (e.g., a devotional, checklist, or guide).
- Stay consistent with your message on social media.
- Engage with your audience — respond to messages, comments, and feedback.

Essential Tools for Speakers

As you grow, you'll need professional materials that reflect your excellence and credibility. These resources—called your speaker assets—help event planners, media, and clients see your value before they even hear your voice.

Core Speaker Assets Include:

- Professional Headshots
- Speaker Bio – a short and long version that highlights your story and expertise
- Signature Talk Description – a brief summary of your main topics or talks
- Speaker One-Sheet – a one-page overview with your photo, bio, topics, audience, and testimonials
- Speaker Reel or Video Clips – short recordings of you speaking to show your delivery and style
- Online Presence – your website, speaker page, or booking link
- Logo or Brand Colors
- High-Quality Testimonials
- Media Kit – for press, podcasts, and collaborations
- Email Pitches – personalized outreach templates to contact event organizers

Building your speaking platform is an act of stewardship, not self-promotion.

It's about packaging your purpose with excellence so your message can reach the people God has assigned to you.

"Excellence attracts opportunities. When you prepare in private, God will showcase you in public."

— Crystal Daye

 **Reflection Questions**

1. What do I want my audience to feel when they encounter my brand?

2. What 3 words describe my speaker style and personality?

3. What values do I want my brand to communicate?

4. How can I make my brand reflect both excellence and authenticity?

5. What speaker assets do I need to develop?

Part 3

The Craft

Chapter 6
DEVELOP YOUR SIGNATURE SPEECH

"Every time you speak, treat it like an assignment, not a performance. You're not just giving a talk — you're delivering transformation."- C. Daye

Every great speaker has a signature speech, the one they could deliver with confidence, clarity, and conviction because it represents who they are and what they stand for. Your signature speech is the talk that captures the heart of your calling. It's the message that becomes your anchor.

What Is a Signature Speech

- It's the **core message** you're known for.
- It's the **talk you can deliver again and again** (with small tweaks) to different audiences.
- It becomes the foundation for your books, workshops, and brand.

Benefits:

- Builds credibility and consistency
- Saves time when preparing for speaking opportunities
- Strengthens your personal brand and income potential

Choosing Your Speaking Topics

Before you craft your speech, you need to identify the core topics you'll be known for. Your topics should align with your purpose, expertise, and audience's needs.

Ask yourself:

- What topics come naturally to me?
- What issues or struggles do I feel called to address?

- Which subjects connect to my testimony or professional experience?
- What conversations am I most passionate about having?

How to Know You've Found the Right Topic:

— You've lived it
— You can teach it with confidence
— People ask you for help or advice about it
— You can connect it to your book, program, or brand
— You could talk about it for 30 minutes — without notes!

Ways to Use Your Signature Talk

1. Use it as the core message of your brand
2. Position yourself as a thought leader
3. Use it for lead generation
4. Turn it into a revenue stream
5. Build trust through storytelling
6. Repurpose it into 90 days of content
7. Refine and improve it through feedback
8. Leverage it to open new opportunities
9. Use it to strengthen your book, coaching, and product offers
10. Use it to build partnerships, collaborations, and media opportunities

The Foundation of Every Great Speech

Once you know your topic, it's time to build your message. Every great speech — whether 10 minutes or an hour — follows a clear flow:

- **Introduction:** Capture attention with a story, quote, or question that connects to your theme
- **Connection:** Build rapport by relating to your audience's pain, dreams, or struggles
- **Content:** Share your key lessons, revelations, framework or strategies (2–3 main points)
- **Call to Action:** Give the audience a way to apply what they've learned — a mindset shift, step, or challenge.

- **Conclusion:** End with power. Summarize your message, cast vision, and leave them inspired.

    "A great speech doesn't give information — it gives transformation."

Writing & Refining Your Speech

- Start by writing out your story, then refine it into key points
- Keep it conversational — speak from your heart, not your notes
- Eliminate filler words and overused clichés
- Practice transitions between points
- Time yourself to ensure your speech fits the length of typical engagements (15, 30, minutes

Deliver with Confidence

- ✓ Prepare spiritually — pray before every event
- ✓ Visualize impact, not perfection
- ✓ Breathe deeply and pause intentionally
- ✓ Engage your audience — make eye contact, ask questions and smile
- ✓ Record your speech and study what works

Naming & Packaging Your Signature Talk

Once you've clarified your main message and chosen your core topic, it's time to give your talk a **powerful name and professional presentation**. A great title should be **clear, catchy, and connected** to your purpose. It should communicate transformation, not just information. When someone hears it, they should instantly feel, *"That's for me."*

Examples

"Faith Over Fear: How to Step Boldly into God's Plan for Your Life"

"Doubt Detox: Renewing Your Mind for a Life of Confidence and Clarity"

"Message to Millions: How to Turn Your Story Into a Movement"

Types of Speaking Platforms

As you develop your signature speech, you'll deliver it across different types of platforms.

Each serves a unique purpose in your growth and visibility.

1. **Other People's Formal Platforms:** Formal platforms build your credibility, authority, and reputation. They help you attract future bookings and higher speaking fees.

These are structured, professional events like:

- Conferences
- Graduations
- Church services
- Corporate trainings
- Retreats or Summits

2. **Other People's Informal Platforms:** Informal platforms help you practice your delivery, refine your message, and build relationships that lead to bigger invitations.

These are smaller but powerful opportunities like:

- Podcasts
- Youth groups
- Online interviews
- Live videos
- YouTube collaborations

3. **Your Own Platforms:** Owning your platform gives you freedom, visibility, and authority. Don't wait for an invitation — create your own! Your own events allow you to share your message freely and build community.

Examples:

- Hosting live or virtual masterclasses
- Organizing workshops or retreats
- Launching a podcast or YouTube channel
- Creating a social media speaking series

"When you can't find a stage—build one. The message God gave you deserves to be heard."

 **Reflection Questions**

1. What is my core speaking topic?

2. Who am I primarily called to serve with this message?

3. What result do I want my audience to experience?

4. Which speaking platforms can I focus on this year?

5. What are your 3 signature talk names?

Chapter 7
THE ART OF STORYTELLING

"When you tell your story, you release someone else from their silence. Your vulnerability becomes the bridge to someone else's victory." – C. Daye

Your story is one of the most powerful tools God has given you to influence others. It's not just a testimony—it's a ministry, a message, and a method for transformation. When you share your story, you're not boasting in your past—you're boasting in His power. You become living proof that God can take broken pieces and build a platform of purpose.

Why Storytelling Matters

Explain the power and purpose of storytelling in ministry and speaking.

- Stories create connection - People may forget your points, but they'll remember your story
- Stories break walls - Vulnerability builds trust faster than information
- Stories make truth relatable - They translate faith into something people can see and feel
- Stories move people to action- They ignite belief that change is possible

How to Overcome the Insecurities to Speak Boldly

Even the most powerful speakers once struggled with fear and self-doubt. You may be thinking, *"Who am I to share my story?"* or *"What if people judge me?"*

Here's the truth—your insecurities are often the exact area God wants to use for impact.

To overcome fear and speak boldly:

- ✓ Remember why you're sharing — it's not about you, it's about who needs your message
- ✓ Focus on service and impact not performance

- ✓ Remind yourself that your story isn't about perfection — it's about process
- ✓ Pray for courage and clarity before you speak
- ✓ Replace "What will they think?" with "Who will this help?"

"You don't need to be fearless to be effective — you just need to be obedient."

How to Use Storytelling as a Speaker

As a speaker, your story is your bridge—it connects truth to transformation. Here's how to use storytelling effectively in your talks:

- ✓ Start your talk with a short, relatable story to capture attention
- ✓ Use mini-stories throughout to illustrate your main points
- ✓ Include the 3V storytelling framework that leaves your audience with hope and clarity
- ✓ Include client stories or testimonies to build credibility and show real results

The 3V Storytelling Framework

Your story doesn't need to be complicated — it just needs to be structured.

Use the **3V Storytelling Framework** to make your message clear and powerful.

The Four Core Phases of the 3V Story:

1. **Victory** — Where are you now? What success or lesson have you achieved?
2. **Valley** — What struggle, challenge, or mistake did you have to overcome?
3. **Pivot** — What changed? What decision, event, or revelation turned it around?
4. **Vision** — What mission or message came out of it? How are you helping others now?

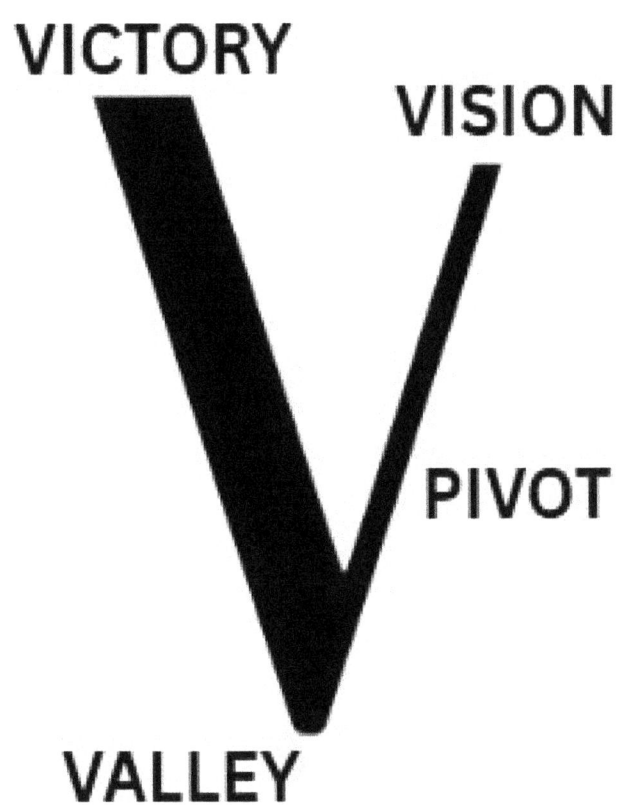

Write Your Signature Story

VICTORY	**VALLEY**

PIVOT	**VISION**

How to Use the 3V Story in Your Talks

This format keeps your story authentic, focused and transformational. To make your 3V story come alive:

- **Start with Victory** → Inspire belief and establish credibility
- **Reveal the Valley** → Build emotional connection and show authenticity
- **Show the Pivot** → Ignite transformation by sharing what changed
- **Share the Vision** → Cast purpose, offer hope, and issue a call to action

Build Your Story Bank

Every speaker should have a Story Bank—a personal library of life experiences, client successes, and lessons learned that can be used for speeches, interviews, books, and online content.

Think of it as your personal treasure chest of transformation moments.

Categories to Include in Your Story Bank:

a) **Growing Up Stories** – Lessons from childhood or early life experiences
b) **Client Success Stories** – Proof of transformation through your message or coaching
c) **Business or Ministry Origin Stories** – How your brand or calling began
d) **Credibility Stories** – Milestones that showcase your expertise or experience
e) **Change in Belief System** – How your mindset or faith evolved
f) **Humor/Funny Stories** – Light-hearted moments that make you relatable
g) **Turning Point/Pivot Stories** – Defining moments that shifted your direction
h) **Failure/Lesson Stories** – Mistakes that taught powerful truths

Tips for Impactful Storytelling

Do:

- ☑ Keep stories short and relevant
- ☑ Speak from scars, not open wounds
- ☑ Practice your pacing, tone, and pauses

- ☑ Always connect your story back to your message
- ☑ Let your emotions guide your delivery—passion persuades

Don't:

- 🚫 Overshare personal trauma without redemption
- 🚫 Make yourself the hero of the story—let God or the lesson shine
- 🚫 Ramble or include unnecessary details
- 🚫 Forget your call to action

"Your vulnerability creates connection but your lesson creates transformation"

Practice, Polish and Protect Your Story

- ✓ Practice your story until it feels natural, not rehearsed
- ✓ Polish it—time it, refine your wording and get feedback
- ✓ Protect it—not everyone deserves every detail. Guard what's sacred.

 **Reflection Questions**

1. What key story from my life best illustrates my message?

2. Which parts of my journey am I still afraid to share, and why?

3. What lesson or transformation do I want my audience to take away?

4. Which of the 3V phases (Victory, Valley, Pivot, Vision) needs more clarity?

5. What 3 stories could I add to my story bank today?

Part 4

The Cashflow

Chapter 8
VISIBILITY AS A PROFESSIONAL SPEAKER

"Visibility is not about being seen by everyone — it's about being found by the ones you're called to reach"
— Crystal Daye

Visibility is not about vanity—it's about stewardship. You can't change lives in rooms you never enter. God didn't give you a message to hide; He gave you a voice to be heard.

As a Kingdom speaker, visibility is about being found by the audience God assigned to you. It's the bridge between calling and impact, between potential and purpose.

"You are the light of the world. A city set on a hill cannot be hidden."
— Matthew 5:14

Why Visibility Matters

- ✓ Visibility multiplies impact
- ✓ Visibility builds credibility
- ✓ Visibility attracts opportunity
- ✓ Visibility allows your message to reach the masses—from stages to screens

How to Position Yourself for Visibility

Being visible starts with positioning—clarity on who you are, what you do, and who you serve.

To position yourself as a professional speaker:

— Know your niche (faith, empowerment, business, leadership, confidence, etc.)
— Define your audience clearly
— Identify your main signature talk(s)
— Create your speaker assets (bio, reel, one-sheet)
— Have a clear message that communicates transformation

The 5 Pillars of Visibility for Kingdom Speakers

These pillars are the foundation that sustains long-term impact and influence.

1. Presence – Where You Show Up

Your presence is how people experience you—both online and offline. It's the energy, confidence, and consistency you bring to every space you enter.

How to Strengthen It:

- Be consistent in showing up — even when you don't feel "ready."
- Cultivate your personal brand voice and message
- Attend events, conferences, and ministry gatherings that align with your vision
- Maintain a positive, professional, and authentic tone online

2. Platform – Where You Speak

Your platform is the space where your message lives and grows. This can be someone else's stage or one you build yourself.

Examples of Platforms:

- ✓ Borrowed: Guest speaking on podcasts, conferences, and online summits.
- ✓ Collaborative: Co-hosting events or joining panel discussions.
- ✓ Owned: Hosting your own events, webinars, YouTube show, or podcast.

3. Publicity – Who's Talking About You

Publicity is about amplification. It's how you expand your reach through others—media, podcasts, magazines, collaborations, or social proof.

Ways to Build Publicity:

- Guest on podcasts
- Submit articles or devotionals to magazines and blogs
- Celebrate your wins and share testimonials
- Use professional photos and media kits to pitch confidently

4. Partnerships – Who You Align With

Strategic partnerships open doors faster than self-promotion ever could.

How to Partner Wisely:

- Build relationships with event planners, media hosts, and other speakers
- Offer value before asking for opportunities
- Collaborate with authors, coaches, or organizations who share your mission
- Support others' platforms—comment, share, and celebrate them

5. Preparation – How You Stay Ready

Preparation is the invisible pillar that holds all others together.

How to Prepare for Greater Visibility:

- ✓ Spend time in prayer before every event, meeting, or stage
- ✓ Keep your bio, reel, and signature talks updated
- ✓ Study your craft — watch other speakers and learn from feedback
- ✓ Prepare your heart: humility sustains what talent begins

"Preparation is the highest act of faith. When you believe God will open doors, you prove it by getting ready"

— **Pray Before and After You Speak**. Remember—it's not just about what you say, but what the Spirit does through what you say.

— **Receive Feedback Humbly.** Growth is part of the journey. Ask for feedback and refine your delivery after every engagement.

How to Find Speaking Engagements (Get Your First Speaking Gig)

If you're just starting your speaking journey, don't wait for invitations—create them. Your first opportunity is often a product of initiative and intention.

Practical Ways to Get Booked:

1. Start Where You Are. Speak at your church, school, community group, or local

events.
2. **Offer Free Value First.** Serve before you sell—volunteer for small groups or workshops to gain experience and exposure.
3. **Leverage Your Network.** Let friends, mentors, and colleagues know you're available to speak.
4. **Pitch Yourself Confidently.** Reach out to event planners, organizations, and podcast hosts with a clear topic and outcome.
5. **Use Social Media.** Post clips, tips, and short videos to showcase your expertise.
6. **Collaborate with Coaches and Authors.** Partner for virtual events or panel discussions.
7. **Host Your Own Event or Webinar.** Don't wait for a platform—build one.
8. **Join Speaker Directories or Associations.** Expand your visibility with professional platforms.
9. **Follow Event Pages and Conferences.** Keep track of call-for-speakers announcements.
10. **Ask for Referrals.** Every time you speak, ask the organizer if they know someone else who needs a speaker.

How to Partner with Event Planners

Event planners are gatekeepers to stages. Building great relationships with them is essential for long-term success.

How to Build Professional Partnerships:

1. **Lead with Value, Not a Pitch:** When reaching out, don't just ask for an opportunity—offer something that adds value to their event or audience.
2. **Show You're Easy to Work With:** Respond promptly, honor deadlines, and be flexible. Planners remember speakers who make their job easier.
3. **Promote the Event Like It's Your Own:** Share graphics, tag the host, and encourage your followers to attend. Planners love speakers who amplify visibility.
4. **Provide Your Speaker Assets:** Have your bio, photo, and session description ready to send.
5. **Collaborate Beyond the Stage:** Stay in touch after the event. Offer to pray for them, share their projects, or refer them to others. Relationships build recurring opportunities.

How to Track & Steward Opportunities

- Keep a simple log or spreadsheet of speaking engagements, contacts, and

feedback.
- Follow up with event hosts after you speak—gratitude builds relationships.
- Collect photos, testimonials, and videos from each event for marketing use.
- Revisit your visibility goals quarterly to assess growth.

 **Reflection Questions**

1. How visible am I right now as a speaker?

2. What's holding me back from being more consistent or confident in showing up?

3. Which platforms or partnerships could help me expand my reach?

4. How can I prepare spiritually and professionally for more opportunities?

5. Which visibility pillar (Presence, Platform, Publicity, Partnership, Preparation) do I need to strengthen most right now?

Chapter 9
MONETIZATION AS A PROFESSIONAL SPEAKER

"Monetization isn't about making money—it's about multiplying your mission. When you get paid for your purpose, you position yourself to impact the world."
— Crystal Daye

Many Kingdom speakers struggle with guilt or fear around money. But charging for your time, wisdom, and expertise doesn't make you less spiritual—it makes you a wise steward.

God doesn't just anoint you to speak—He calls you to steward your voice. That means learning how to package your message in a way that brings transformation and financial increase.

You are not just a messenger—you are a marketplace minister.

"A worker is worthy of his wages." — Luke 10:7

Monetization isn't about greed—it's about growth. It's how you expand your capacity to serve, give, and sustain your assignment long-term.

The Speaker Business Flow

Turning your message into a business means moving from passion to process.

1. CRAFT YOUR MESSAGE → Define your story, framework, and expertise
2. BUILD YOUR ASSETS → Bio, speaker reel, one-sheet, slides, and professional photos
3. MARKET YOUR BRAND → Show up consistently online and offline; build relationships
4. MONETIZE YOUR PLATFORM → Create paid offers, packages, and products
5. MANAGE YOUR BUSINESS → Track bookings, invoices, and client relationships

"When you treat your speaking like a business, it starts paying like one."

How to Set Fees and Increase Your Earnings as a Speaker

Every professional speaker must learn to confidently charge for their time, experience, and transformation. You are not being paid for an hour on stage—you're being paid for years of study, storytelling, and skill.

Here's how to start setting your speaker fees confidently:

1. Start with your experience: If you're just starting, you may accept lower fees or free opportunities to build your reputation—but always do so strategically (not from fear).
2. Research standard rates: Look at industry averages and local speaker benchmarks. Start with a baseline rate and increase it as your brand grows.
3. Factor in your preparation and expertise: Include the time it takes to prepare your slides, travel, and follow-ups.
4. Add value-based pricing: Your rate should reflect the outcome you deliver—not just the minutes you speak.
5. Review your pricing every 12 months based on demand: As your demand, credibility, and audience grow, your prices should too.

Pro Tip: Always offer tiered options (e.g., keynote, breakout session, or full-day training) so clients can choose based on budget and value.

"Don't shrink your value to fit someone's budget — expand your vision to attract someone who values your worth."

Using Speaking to Build Your Business

Speaking is one of the most powerful ways to grow your business or ministry. Every stage becomes an opportunity to sell books, attract coaching clients, or expand your audience.

Ways to use your speaking platform to grow your business:

- Offer a free resource or QR code at the end of your talk to capture leads
- Share your book or signature coaching program naturally within your talk
- Host a booth or table to sell your resources after your session
- Mention your social media or website for follow-up
- Partner with event hosts to offer a bonus session or group program

Creating Multiple Streams of Income as a Speaker

Don't limit your income to honorariums. Your voice can open multiple financial doors—if you package it right.

Here are some ways to create income streams from your message:

- Host your own live or virtual events. Create workshops, summits, or retreats around your topic.
- Develop audio or video courses. Teach your framework once and sell it repeatedly. Create coaching programs. Offer one-on-one or group coaching tied to your speaking topics.
- Sell books and journals. Every event is an opportunity for book sales or bulk orders.
- Collaborate with other brands or speakers. Co-host programs or events that expand your reach.

Speaking for Free vs Speaking for a Fee

As you grow your speaking career, you'll receive both paid and unpaid invitations. The key is learning to discern when to say "yes" strategically—and when to say "no" wisely. Not all free stages are bad, and not all paid stages are worth it. You must choose opportunities that align with your purpose, positioning, and profit goals.

When to Speak for Free (Strategically)

Speaking for free can still be profitable if it helps you grow visibility, credibility, or opportunity.

- ❖ The audience is your ideal client or target audience.
- ❖ You can sell books, courses, or coaching programs at the event.
- ❖ You're building your portfolio or stage experience.
- ❖ You'll receive high-quality photos or videos for marketing.
- ❖ The platform gives you access to media coverage or collaboration.
- ❖ It aligns with your mission or ministry—and you feel led by purpose, not pressure.

How to Transition from Free to Fee

- ❖ Start speaking for free strategically. Collect testimonials, footage, and experience.
- ❖ Create a Speaker Rate Sheet. Include packages like Keynote, Workshop, Panel, or Virtual.
- ❖ Pitch and negotiate confidently. You bring value—don't be afraid to discuss payment.
- ❖ Set clear policies for waiving your fee. Only do so for purpose-led, mission-aligned events. Always monetize the moment. Even if the stage doesn't pay, your audience might (through product sales, email signups, or coaching leads).

How to Sell From the Stage Authentically

- ❖ Tell stories that illustrate the need for your product or service.
- ❖ Give a clear call to action at the end ("If you were inspired today, here's your next step..."). Offer bonuses or bundles at events.
- ❖ Always make it easy to purchase (QR code, order form, or table setup).
- ❖ Pray before you present any offer—God will align hearts.

"Selling is serving—you're simply giving people a way to go deeper."

How to Steward Your Finances as a Speaker

- Tithe and give generously
- Save a portion of your income
- Reinvest in professional development (courses, coaches, media kits)
- Budget for travel and marketing
- Pay taxes

 **Reflection Questions**

1. What fears or beliefs have held me back from charging what you're worth?

2. Where can I speak this quarter to reach my ideal audience?

3. How can I serve more people and still steward my energy and finances well?

4. What's one new way I can monetize my message this quarter?

5. Do you have a system for tracking and following up with clients?

Chapter 10
HOW TO SELL YOUR BOOKS AS A SPEAKER

"Every speech is a seed — and your book is the harvest"

When God gave you the message for your book, He didn't intend for it to sit on a shelf, He meant for it to change lives. And one of the most powerful ways to expand your book's reach is by using your voice.

As a speaker, your message comes alive in real time. When people connect with you emotionally from the stage, they naturally want to take that message home—and that's what your book does.

The Connection Between Speaking and Selling

When you speak, you build trust. When people trust you, they buy from you. That's why some of your biggest book sales will come after you speak.

Your talk allows the audience to experience your story, personality, and authority—and that connection leads to conversion.

Think of it this way:

- Your voice creates the emotional connection
- Your book provides the continued transformation

Positioning Your Book in Your Talk

The key is to integrate your book naturally into your presentation—not as a sales pitch, but as a part of your purpose.

How to Mention Your Book Gracefully:

— Use stories or lessons from your book to illustrate key points
— Reference it in a way that feels authentic ("In my book, I share how God walked me through...")
— Display the book visually during your talk

— Add it to your slides or presentation graphics
— Include your book title in your speaker introduction or bio

"If your message changes lives, your book is a tool for transformation—not a transaction."

How to Sell Books Before, During, and After You Speak

Before the Event:

- Offer bulk book packages to the organizer (include books for all attendees).
- Include your book in your speaker proposal or package.
- Send them a media kit or bundle offer: "Keynote + 50 books = discounted rate."
- Announce upcoming events to your email list and social media followers to pre-sell copies.

During the Event:

- Have a book table or assistant ready to handle sales.
- Offer bundle deals (e.g., "Buy 2, get 1 free" or "Book + journal").
- Share a powerful excerpt from your book as part of your speech.
- Use QR codes or mobile payment options for easy checkout.
- Encourage selfies or photos with your book for online buzz.

After the Event:

- Collect emails from book buyers and follow up with gratitude notes.
- Send a discount or bonus for leaving reviews.
- Ask the event host for feedback and referrals.
- Post event highlights with your book on social media.

Packaging Your Book With Your Speaking Offers

Your book adds tangible value to your speaking packages and positions you as an expert.

Ways to Package Your Book With Your Speaking:

- Keynote Bundle: Book + 50 signed copies for attendees
- Workshop Bundle: Book + workbook or journal + training session
- Virtual Bundle: Book + online course + bonus session
- Corporate/Church Package: Include books in ticket or registration fees

"When you combine your book and your voice, you multiply your impact and income."

How to Use Your Book to Book More Speaking Gigs

Your book is your best marketing tool as a speaker. It's proof of your credibility, clarity, and consistency.

Ways Your Book Opens Doors:

- Send copies to event planners or decision-makers with a handwritten note.
- Include it as part of your media or speaker kit.
- Use it as leverage when pitching conferences and podcasts.
- Mention it when networking — "I actually wrote a book about that!"
- Turn chapters into workshops, devotionals, or talk topics.

Practical Tips for On-the-Spot Sales

- Always travel with at least 10–20 copies of your book.
- Keep digital payment options (CashApp, Zelle, PayPal, Square).
- Have a simple sign-up sheet for your email list.
- Bring table decor and book stands for a professional look.
- Have postcards or bookmarks to hand out (even if people don't buy).
- Capture photos and testimonials with readers holding your book.

What To Do If You Don't Have a Book Yet

Don't worry—you don't need a published book to start building your speaking platform.

In fact, many powerful speakers spoke their message long before they ever wrote it.

The truth is, your message is already inside you. The book is just the next container that will carry it further. So while you're preparing to write, here's how to start positioning yourself now:

1. Speak From Your Story: Start sharing the core message or testimony that your future book will be based on. Your story builds connection, and your voice builds credibility. Don't wait until the book is done—let your message start working for you now.

2. Start Collecting Content Now: Use your talks, live videos, podcast interviews, and even social media posts as building blocks for your future book. These moments will become chapters later.

    a) Record your speeches and transcribe them later.
    b) Keep a running document titled "Book Notes" or "Talks to Chapters."
    c) Journal your audience's reactions—what topics make them light up?

3. Build Your Email List and Community: Even without a book, you can start building an audience that's excited to read it once it's released. When your book launches, these are the same people who'll buy, share, and promote it for you.

    a) Offer a free resource (e.g., "7 Faith Steps to Finding Your Voice") in exchange for emails.
    b) Stay consistent with newsletters, devotionals, or weekly encouragements.
    c) Use every speaking event to invite people to join your community.

4. Use Speaking to Refine Your Book Message: Each time you speak, you're testing and shaping the message of your future book. Those are the exact topics your readers will need in print later.

Pay attention to:

- What stories resonate most with the audience,
- Which parts of your talk spark questions, tears, or "aha" moments, and
- What people keep asking you about afterward.

5. Create a Short Resource First: If you're not ready for a full-length book, start smaller. This not only builds credibility but also gives audiences something tangible

to take home while you work on your full book.

- Write a short devotional or 21-day journal
- Create an eBook or mini-guide based on your message
- Design a digital workbook that supports your speech

6. Partner With a Publisher or Coach Early: If you already know you'll write a book, start connecting with publishing experts early.

They can help you:

- Map your message clearly
- Build a realistic writing and publishing timeline
- Avoid mistakes that first-time authors make

Note: At DayeLight Publishers, we guide Kingdom authors from idea to impact—helping you write, publish, promote and monetize books that change lives.

7. Stay Obedient to the Process: Don't let comparison or impatience make you feel behind. God's timing for your book is perfect. Right now, your job is to stay faithful with the message you already have—and keep speaking until the next instruction comes.

Reflection Questions

1. How can I include my book naturally in my next talk?

2. What systems do you have in place for selling books at events?

3. How can I package my speaking and book offers for maximum value?

4. How can you make every talk lead to more transformation and more sales?

Resources

Event Preparation Checklist

Spiritual Preparation

— Before you prepare your slides, prepare your spirit.
— Pray over the event, host, and audience.
— Study and meditate on your anchor Scripture.
— Declare affirmations like "My voice carries purpose and power".
— Write down your faith goal—what you want your audience to walk away with.

Message Preparation

— Review your talk outline and key points.
— Practice your opening and closing stories.
— Time your presentation to stay within the limit.
— Print or save your notes (cue cards, tablet, or PDF) Review Scriptures, quotes, or statistics for accuracy. Rehearse your talk at least twice out loud.

Brand & Materials

— Your presentation is part of your brand—make sure you show up polished and professional.
— Print copies of your speaker bio and introduction for the host.
— Pack business cards or a QR code that links to your website or booking page.
— Prepare your book table setup (books, journals, payment tools, tablecloth, pens).
— Have 3-5 talking points ready in case of interviews.

Logistics & Personal Prep

— Set yourself up for a smooth experience—peace before presentation. Confirm event details (location, date, time, audience size).
— Check your travel arrangements and arrival time.
— Coordinate your outfit—comfortable, confident, and camera-ready.
— Pack backup items (lipstick, tissues, flat shoes, deodorant, charger, etc.)
— Stay hydrated and rest the night before.
— Arrive early for mic checks, prayer, and to greet the host.

Engagement & Follow-Up

— Your impact extends beyond the stage—steward the moment well.
— Connect with the audience before and after your talk.
— Smile and make eye contact—let them feel your authenticity.
— Collect testimonials, photos, or video clips for marketing.
— Thank the organizer and their team personally.
— Send a "thank you" email or note within 48 hours.
— Post highlights and gratitude online to share the impact.

Crystal Daye

Empowering | Transparent | Passionate

Speaker, Book Coach, Publisher, Talk Show & Podcast Host

✉️ crystalsdaye@gmail.com

in linkedin.com/in/crystalsdaye/

About Me

Crystal Daye is a kingdom entrepreneur, author of 10 books, sought after inspirational speaker, and Certified Christian Master coach. Growing up in poverty and being told she will never be successful; Crystal became resolute to not settle for mediocrity but instead she uses her story to impact lives globally.

After living a life of partying, poverty, promiscuity, being abused and struggling with feelings of insecurity, she encountered Jesus Christ in the midst of her brokenness. Since then, Crystal has committed to living a life of faith, obedience and purpose. She now passionately empowers women to deepen their intimacy with God, discover their identity and use their message to impact lives.

Crystal is the CEO of DayeLight Publishers, Host of The DayeLight Talk Show aired on MTM Tv, Host of the Ambitious Jesus Girl Podcast and Founder of Empowering Girls Club. Crystal's practical anecdotes, vibrant personality, real-life stories and biblical insight keeps her in constant demand as a speaker and mentor. She has been featured in multiple television, radio, podcasts, magazines and publications locally and internationally.

Speaking Topics

- Brand New Free: Walking In True Freedom in Christ
- GoodBye Insecurity, Hello Impact: Walk Boldly In Your God-Given Gifts
- Faithpreneur Secrets: How To Build A Thriving Business Without Compromising Your Faith

As Seen On/In

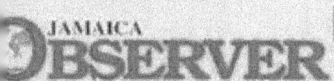

Booking Information

Available to speak at Conferences, Retreats, Workshop, Panel, Seminars and Podcast Interviews

🌐 www.crystalsdaye.com
✉️ crystalsdaye@gmail.com
📞 876-540-4863

SWOT Analysis For Speakers

When I studied business, I was introduced to a tool called the SWOT Analysis—a simple yet powerful framework used to make wise decisions about where to invest and how to grow as an entrepreneur. And guess what? The same principle applies to your speaking career.

As a Kingdom speaker, understanding your Strengths, Weaknesses, Opportunities, and Threats (SWOT) helps you make smarter decisions about how to build, position and expand your platform.

This analysis gives you a clear picture of what's working for you, what areas need development, and what opportunities (or obstacles) exist in the marketplace.

Why Every Speaker Should Do a SWOT Analysis

Whether you're just starting out or already booking engagements, a SWOT helps you:

- ☑ Evaluate how marketable your message is
- ☑ Identify growth areas in your delivery, branding, or audience reach
- ☑ Discover new opportunities for visibility and income
- ☑ Build confidence through self-awareness and preparation

For Example:

S – Strengths: Passionate storyteller, Confident stage presence, Deep knowledge of your topic
W – Weaknesses: Nervousness or fear before speaking, Weak time management, Limited marketing, Inconsistent online presence
O – Opportunities: Growing demand for speakers, Local schools or churches hosting regular events, Virtual platforms seeking guests
T – Threats: Market saturation, Limited budgets, Comparison and imposter syndrome

Strengths
(abilities, experience, knowledge, credentials)

Weaknesses
(knowledge, skills, money, help you need)

Threats
(market, competition, external obstacles)

Opportunities
(market, need, partnership, ease of entry)

90-Day Goal Planner For Speakers

The purpose of a 90-day plan is to help you focus on what matters now. Instead of being overwhelmed by a full year of goals, this planner guides you to break your big vision into clear, strategic 90-day stretches.

Your 90-day plan will only work if you know exactly what you want and why you want it—so dream big, write boldly, and plan with intention.

Here are some examples of what your speaker goals are (go over the 4 types of goals in Chapter 3)

- Share my testimony to inspire healing in women. Eliminate filler words by practicing weekly.
- Book 3–5 paid speaking engagements.
- Sell 200 books from speaking events for the year. Post weekly speaking content online.
- Pitch myself to five podcasts.

90 DAY GOAL PLANNER

90 Days from today is: _____

My main goal is

Why do you want to accomplish this goal? (What will happen?) DREAM BIG!

Write an "I see myself" affirmation about achieving this goal.
I see myself

Who will be your accountability partner?

Let's Get To Werk☺

© 2017, DayeLight International

Section 1: Break Down Your 90 Day Plan

Based on my major goal, my top 3 goals for these 90 days are:

Goal #1:

Actions I will take to reach this goal:

Goal #2:

Actions I will take to reach this goal:

Goal #3:

Actions I will take to reach this goal:

© 2017, DayeLight International

Section 2: Top Priorities to help with goals

Top 3 Priorities are:

Other important stuff to get done:

Make your own rules to help you stay productive during these 90 days:

© 2017, DayeLight International

Section 3: How I will measure my progress

Once I start working on my plan, I need to measure my progress. This will keep me on track and help me identify any problems as soon as they arise.

<u>30-Day Progress:</u>

Date:

My progress to date:

I am on track and on time toward achieving my goal.   YES   NO

If not, I will modify my plan to accomplish my goal by:

<u>60-Day Progress:</u>

Date:

My progress to date:

I am on track and on time toward achieving my goal.   YES   NO

If not, I will modify my plan to accomplish my goal by:

<u>30-Day Progress:</u>

Date:

My progress to date:

I am on track and on time toward achieving my goal.   YES   NO

If not, I will modify my plan to accomplish my goal by:

© 2017, DayeLight International

Section 4: Motivation Reminders

- Time is short—take action now. Your calling requires movement.
- Be positive. Be consistent. Be motivated.
- Identify your distractions and create boundaries.
- Visualize the speaker God is shaping you to become.
- Give thanks daily and pray without ceasing.
- The world needs your voice.
- Make your goals a daily priority.
- You don't "find" time—**you make time**.
- Discipline is required to achieve greatness.
- God wants you to prosper and walk boldly in your purpose.

© 2017, DayeLight International

About the Author

Crystal Daye is an international speaker, bestselling author and one of the Caribbean's leading voices in faith-based personal and professional development. As a Kingdom Entrepreneur and CEO of DayeLight Publishers, she has become a premier authority on helping emerging leaders transform their stories, their message, and their voice into platforms that inspire, influence, and impact lives.

With over two decades of experience on international stages—churches, conferences, corporations, women's summits, educational institutions, and global virtual platforms—Crystal has delivered life-shifting messages to thousands across the world. She is known for her dynamic storytelling, faith-filled teaching, and ability to help purpose-driven women speak with clarity, confidence, and conviction.

Under her leadership, DayeLight Publishers has become the Caribbean's top faith-based publishing and author development company—guiding writers from concept to published book and empowering them to use speaking as a strategic tool for global influence.

Crystal is deeply passionate about helping women of faith discover their identity in Christ, break free from insecurity, and boldly walk in their calling. Whether through her books, live events, coaching programs, or her widely loved podcast "Reaching Millions," she equips believers to amplify their voice, elevate their platform, and monetize their message without compromising their Kingdom values.

For speaking engagements, coaching, or corporate faith-based training, contact Crystal at info@crystaldaye.com or visit www.crystaldaye.com or www.dayelightpublishers.com.

Connect with Crystal:
Instagram: @crystalsdaye @dayelightpublishers Facebook: @crystalsdaye @dayelightpublishers LinkedIn: @crystaldaye

Books by Crystal Daye

DAYELIGHT PUBLISHERS

THIS IS A FAITH-BASED PUBLISHING CONSULTANCY COMPANY THAT IS COMMITTED TO HELPING ASPIRING AUTHORS AND KINGDOM LEADERS THROUGH THE PROCESS OF HOW TO WRITE, PUBLISH, BRAND AND MARKET THEIR BOOK

SERVICES OFFERED:

- BOOK COACHING
- EDITORIAL & PROOFREADING
- KINDLE & PAPERBACK FORMATTING
- SELF PUBLISHING CONSULTANCY
- BOOK COVER DESIGN & GRAPHIC DESIGNS
- WORLDWIDE BOOK DISTRIBUTION
- ISBN & BARCODE ACQUISITION
- BOOK MARKETING & PROMOTIONAL ASSISTANCE
- SERMONS TO BOOK
- WEBSITE DEVELOPMENT
- BRAND & BUSINESS CONSULTANCY

CRYSTAL DAYE
AWARD-WINNING AUTHOR, BOOK COACH & CHIEF PUBLISHING OFFICER

www.dayelightpublishers.com   info@dayelightpublishers.com

WE ARE A GUIDING AGENT TO GET YOUR BOOK OUT THE IDEAL READERS AND WE ARE NOT HERE FOR OWNERSHIP, SO YOU KEEP 100% OF YOUR ROYALTIES!

www.ingramcontent.com/pod-product-compliance
Lightning Source LLC
Chambersburg PA
CBHW050455110426
42743CB00017B/3374